Artisans Around the World

North America

Mary Tull, Sharon Franklin, and Cynthia A. Black

RSVP

RAINTREE
STECK-VAUGHN
P U B L I S H E R S
A Steck-Vaughn Company

Austin, Texas

www.steck-vaughn.com

Developed by Franklin Tull, Inc.,
Manager: Sharon Franklin
Designer: Dahna Solar
Maps: Terragraphics, Inc.
Illustrators: Dahna Solar and James Cloutier
Picture Researcher: Mary Tull
Projects: Cynthia A. Black

Raintree Steck-Vaughn Publishers Staff
Project Manager: Joyce Spicer
Editor: Pam Wells
Electronic Production: Scott Melcer

Photo Credits: CORBIS/Joel W. Rogers: p. 8LR; Courtesy of the Museum of Anthropology at the University of British Columbia: pp. 8UL, 8UR, 10UR, 13UR; David N. Olsen/The Stock Solution: p. 8LL; CORBIS/Dewitt Jones: pp. 9L, 11LR; Bruce Hucko: pp. 11CL, 14LL; Uli Steltzer: p. 12UL; Charles Rhyne: p. 12LR; CORBIS/©Werner Forman: p. 13LL; Bernard Hehl/Unicorn Stock Photos: p. 18UL; Michael Philip Manheim/The Stock Solution: p. 18UR; Don Eastman/The Stock Solution: p. 18LL; Kutztown Pennsylvania German Festival/Unger's Studio: pp. 18LR, 19UR, 20UL, 21UL; Reading & Berks County Visitors Bureau: p. 19LR; Library of Congress: p. 20UR; Jim Shippee/Unicorn Stock Photos: p. 21LR; Jacob Zook original hex signs courtesy of Will Char, The Hex Place, Paradise, PA: p. 22; Daemmrich/The Stock Solution: p.26UL; Tom Till/The Stock Solution: pp. 26UR, 36LL; Robert W. Ginn/The Stock Solution: p. 26LL; CORBIS/Richard A. Cooke: p. 26LR; Ron Ruehl, Significance Communications: pp. 27LL, 28UR, 28CR, 30LL, 30UR; Harry DeLorme, Telfair Museum of Art, Savannah, Georgia, Arthur Peter Dilbert at Work: p. 27LR; John Hall, Walking Stick with Eagle's Head, 1996, carved cedar: Telfair Museum of Art, Savannah, Georgia, Museum Purchase, 1997, Photo: Erwin Gaspin Photography, Savannah, Georgia: p. 29LL; Vernon Edwards, "Highlander" Rattlesnake Cane, 1990, Telfair Museum of Art, Savannah, Georgia, Museum Purchase, 1997, Photo: Erwin Gaspin Photography, Savannah, Georgia: p. 29LC; Vernon Edwards at Work: Photo Harry DeLorme, Telfair Museum of Art, Savannah, Georgia: p. 29LR; Vernon Edwards, Frederick Douglass, 1982, Mahogany, Telfair Museum of Art, Savannah, Georgia, Museum Purchase 1997, Photo credit: Erwin Gaspin Photography, Savannah, Georgia: p. 30LR; David R. Frazier/The Stock Solution: p. 34UL; Scott T. Smith/The Stock Solution: pp. 34CL, 36L; Stan Osolinski/The Stock Solution: p. 34LR; Bruce Hucko: pp. 34CR, 38LL, 39LL, 39LR, 40UL, 40LL; Bachmann/The Stock Solution: p. 35LR; Gary Tepfer: pp. 36UR, 37CL, 40UR; CORBIS/Joel W. Rogers: p. 40LR. All project photos by James Cloutier. [**Photo credit key:** First Letter: U-Upper; C-Center, L-Lower; Second letter: R-Right; L-Left]

Library of Congress Cataloging-in-Publication Data
Tull, Mary.
    North America / Mary Tull, Sharon Franklin, and Cynthia A. Black.
        p.   cm. — (Artisans around the world)
    Includes bibliographical references and index.
    Summary: Describes the cultures historically found among the Haida Indians of the Queen Charlotte Islands, the German settlers of Pennsylvania, the Cherokee and African Americans of the Southern United States, and the Pueblo of New Mexico, and provides instructions for projects that introduce their crafts.
    ISBN 0-7398-0117-1
    1. Indian craft — Juvenile literature. 2. Indians of North America — Art — Juvenile literature. 3. Indians of North America — Social life and customs — Juvenile literature. [1. Indian craft. 2. Handicraft. 3. Indians of North America — Social life and customs. 4. Pennsylvania Dutch — Social life and customs.] I. Franklin, Sharon. II. Black, Cynthia A. III. Title. IV. Series.
TT22.T85   1999
745.5'097 — dc21

98-49507
CIP   AC

Table of Contents

The icons next to the projects in the Table of Contents identify the easiest and the most challenging project in the book. This may help you decide which project to do first.

⇨ easiest project

✪ most challenging project

Introduction to Artisans Around the World

There are many ways to learn about the history and present-day life of people in other countries. In school, students often study the history of a country to learn about its people. In this series, you will learn about the history, geography, and the way of life of groups of people through their folk art. People who create folk art are called **artisans.** They are skilled in an art, a craft, or a trade. You will then have a chance to create your own folk art, using your own ideas and symbols.

What Is Folk Art?

Folk art is not considered "fine art." Unlike many fine artists, folk artisans do not generally go to school to learn how to do their art. Very few folk artists are known as "famous" outside of their countries or even their towns. Folk art is the art of everyday people of a region. In this series, folk art also includes primitive art, that is, the art of the first people to be in an area. But, beware! Do not let this fool you into thinking that folk art is not "real" art. As you will see, the quality of the folk art in this series is amazing by any standards.

Folk art comes from the heart and soul of common people. It is an expression of their feelings. Often, it shows their personal, political, or religious beliefs. It may also have a practical purpose or meet a specific need, such as the need for shelter. In many cases, the folk art in the "Artisans Around the World" series comes from groups of people who did not even have a word for art in their culture. Art was simply what people did. It was a part of being human.

Introduction to *North America*

In this book, you will learn about these crafts and the people who do them:

Button blankets in the Queen Charlotte Islands

Hex signs in Pennsylvania

Woodcarving in the Southern United States

Coiled pottery in New Mexico

Then you will learn how to do projects of your own.

Here are some questions to think about as you read this book:

Which of these folk arts helped to meet people's needs?

Which folk arts expressed people's religious, political, or personal views?

Were some of these folk arts traditionally created mostly by men or by women?
Why do you think that was so? Is it still true today?

How did the history of a country influence some folk art traditions?

How did the geography, including the natural resources, of a country
influence some folk art traditions? How did people get folk art materials that
they needed but that were not found in their region?

Do some folk art traditions tell a story about a group of people or a culture?
If so, in what way?

How have these folk art traditions been passed down from generation to generation?

Folk Art Today

Reading about these folk art traditions, as well as creating your own folk art,
will increase your respect for the people who first did them. Do you think some of these
art forms, such as button blankets, could be created faster or more easily using machines,
like the sewing machine, or technology, like the computer?
Do you think anything would be lost by doing so, even if it were possible?

All of these folk art traditions of North America began long ago.
Can you think of any new folk art traditions being started now, in the
United States or in other countries? If so, what are they?
If not, why do you think there are no new traditions?

Safety Guidelines

These folk art projects are a lot of fun to do, but it's important to follow basic safety rules
as you work. Here are some guidelines to help as you complete the projects in this book.
Work slowly and carefully. That way you can enjoy the process.

1. Part of being a responsible person of any age is knowing when to ask for help. Some
   of these projects are challenging. Ask an adult for help whenever you need it. Even
   where the book does not tell you to, feel free to ask for help if you need it.

2. Handle all pointed tools, such as scissors, in a safe manner. Keep them stored in a safe
   place when not in use.

3. When painting, protect your clothing with an old shirt or a smock. When wet, acrylic
   paint can be removed with water. After it dries, it cannot be removed.

4. Woodworking Safety
   • You must have an adult work with you. Ask an adult to do any sawing or trimming.
   • Learn the correct way to use a tool, and use it for its intended purpose only.
   • Use common sense! Cut away from yourself and others.
   • Do not force or jam the tool into the wood. Let the tool do the work.
   • Always clamp the wood to a stable base before sawing or drilling.
   • Put tools away when you are finished with them.

5. Clay Safety
   • Clean your worktable with a wet sponge before the clay dries.
   • Clover your clothes with a smock. Wash the smock when you are finished working.
   • Wear a dust mask when you are sanding or smoothing dry clay.

6. Stain Safety
   • Wear a dust mask when you mix stains.
   • Work in a well-ventilated area.
   • Don't eat while you are working with stains.
   • Avoid skin and eye contact.
   • Clean your worktable well when you are finished working.

By the way, part of being an artist involves cleaning up! Be sure to clean up your work area
when you are finished. Also, remember to thank anyone who helped you.

Hydaburg

A L A S K A

Kaigani Haida

Prince of Wales Island

UNITED STATES

CANADA

Dixon Entrance

A Haida woodcarver works on carving a totem pole. Button blankets have been called "totem poles on cloth."

Haida celebrations include music and dance. Drums set the rhythm as Haida people dance in their ceremonial button blanket robes.

Old Masset (Haida)

Graham Island

Prince Rupert

BRITISH COLUMBIA

Masset Inlet Port Clements

QUEEN CHARLOTTE ISLANDS

(HAIDA GWAII)

Central Highlands

Hecate Strait

Skidegate

Skidegate Inlet

Moresby Island

The black bear lives in the Queen Charlotte Islands and in British Columbia. It is the most common bear in North America.

PACIFIC OCEAN

Gwaii Hanas National Park Reserve

Juan Perez Sound

Over 150 separate islands make up the Queen Charlotte Islands (Haida Gwaii).

N
W E
S

0   50 miles
0   50 km

Queen Charlotte Sound

Queen Charlotte Islands

Origin of the Islands

Geologists believe that, between 200 million and 160 million years ago, underwater volcanic eruptions formed the base of the Queen Charlotte Islands. Later, sandstone and **shale** were deposited in the shallow sea. Some of the shale lay near a volcanic mountain chain that was slowly forming. This chain would become the spine of the Queen Charlotte Islands and home to the Haida Indians.

Arriving at Graham

The Queen Charlotte Islands are a remote **archipelago** of over 150 islands off the northern coast of British Columbia. The southern islands, including Moresby, are very mountainous. Graham, the large northern island, is now home to the Haida people. Hecate Strait lies between the mainland and the islands. It is known as one of the wildest bodies of water in the world. The Haida were masters of these treacherous waters.

Today, most tourists choose to cross the strait by ferries or by air. Even by air the trip can be challenging. It is a 40-minute flight from Prince Rupert to Graham. First, the seaplane picks its way through driftwood in the harbor. The plane slowly rises, rocked by strong gusts of wind. Thick fog and heavy rain make it very hard to see. Finally, islands and ocean appear, just in time to touch ground at Masset Harbor. The native Haida village, Old Masset, is a short distance away. Once, tidy rows of Haida houses and giant totem poles could be seen. Today, few of those structures remain. Still, this village of 1,000 represents the largest Haida population anywhere in the world today.

Haida dancers' masks rest on ▶ driftwood on the beach on Graham Island. Masks represent spirits and are used in ceremonies by both men and women.

A Proud and Prosperous People

For centuries, the Haida were well-protected by their remote location and the forbidding seas. They were a proud people who lived in harmony with nature. The land and sea resources and freshwater streams provided plenty to eat. They built sturdy homes from cedar planks. The Haida were excellent canoe builders and woodcarvers. Their stable food supply allowed them to create permanent villages. It also gave them time to develop their art.

▲ This drawing of the inside of a Haida house is based on early accounts of people visiting the village.

Europeans Arrive

The Haida were generous and welcoming to visitors, especially European explorers and traders. Unfortunately, in the 1860s, these visitors brought diseases which killed more than 90 percent of the Haida population. Those who did not die were met by missionaries who arrived in 1876. The missionaries discouraged Haida songs, dances, and the wearing of ceremonial robes, or **button blankets.** In 1880, it became a crime to participate in a **potlatch,** the Haida's most important ceremony. Totem poles were cut down. Haida children were sent away to distant schools where they were forbidden to speak their native language. By the time they returned, many of them were strangers in their own villages.

"People of the Islands"

The word Haida means "people." Haida legends and archaeological discoveries suggest that the Haida have inhabited these islands since the end of the last Ice Age. This makes the Haida one of the oldest traceable populations in North America.

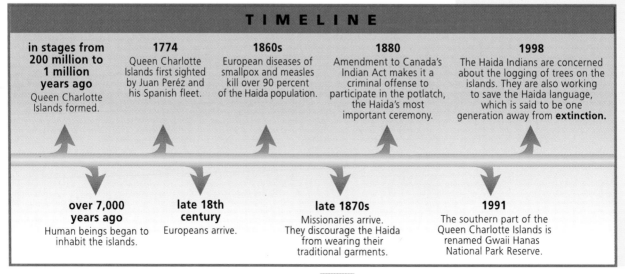

TIMELINE

in stages from 200 million to 1 million years ago
Queen Charlotte Islands formed.

1774
Queen Charlotte Islands first sighted by Juan Peréz and his Spanish fleet.

1860s
European diseases of smallpox and measles kill over 90 percent of the Haida population.

1880
Amendment to Canada's Indian Act makes it a criminal offense to participate in the potlatch, the Haida's most important ceremony.

1998
The Haida Indians are concerned about the logging of trees on the islands. They are also working to save the Haida language, which is said to be one generation away from **extinction.**

over 7,000 years ago
Human beings began to inhabit the islands.

late 18th century
Europeans arrive.

late 1870s
Missionaries arrive. They discourage the Haida from wearing their traditional garments.

1991
The southern part of the Queen Charlotte Islands is renamed Gwaii Hanas National Park Reserve.

Raven and Eagle

The Haida are divided into two social groups, or clans, called Raven and Eagle. All villages contain both Raven and Eagle clan members. Songs, legends, dances, and **crests,** or symbolic designs, are all passed down through the mother's clan. They are respected pieces of property that are owned by the clan.

Crests

Most Haida objects, including carvings, button blankets, and totem poles are decorated with crests. One Haida woman explains that a crest is like your name. Wherever you go, your crest lets people know where you are from. They will know who your relatives are.

The Raven and Eagle clans each have their own crests. It is a great privilege to be given a crest to wear. Both Raven and Eagle clans use the Killer Whale crest. When used by Raven clan members, the Killer Whale's tall dorsal fin is always black. A diagonal white stripe on the dorsal fin identifies it as belonging to an Eagle clan member. Most sea mammal and all land mammal crests, except Beaver, belong to the Ravens. Only Eagles use Beaver and Frog crests.

▲ Raven represents one of two Haida clans. In Haida mythology Raven brings the light.

Haida elders dress in full ceremonial button blanket robes at the dedication of a new canoe. Each robe displays the wearer's individual crest.

▲ Haida artist Robert Davidson helps keep Haida traditions and culture alive.

Totem Poles

Totem poles display personal crests. They document events in the life of a Haida family, a village, or the Haida people.

Carving a totem pole takes a lot of time and energy. Red cedar trunks are usually used, because of their height and size. Red cedar has a straight grain and is easy to carve. Sometimes designs are drawn directly onto the pole using stencils. At other times, a model is carved before the full-sized totem pole is started.

The Potlatch

The potlatch was, and still is, a very important and sacred ceremony among the Haida and other Northwest Coast Indians. Potlatches mark the giving of names, marriages, deaths, and the raising of totem poles. At a potlatch, people dance, feast, and observe rituals for several days. It is also an occasion for giving to other people items of great value.

It takes years to prepare for a potlatch. Village families work hard to make fine button blankets, totem poles, and other handicrafts. At a traditional naming ceremony, the one who is named receives a special button blanket decorated with the family crest. When a person receives a name and a crest, it is a great honor. It means that he or she is entitled to the songs and other things that are a part of that name and crest.

This totem pole, titled *Killer Whales and Wolves,* was carved by Robert Davidson. His Haida name is ǥuud san glans, Robert Davidson, which means "Eagle of the Dawn."

Before the introduction ▶
of cloth by Europeans in the
1700s, Haida blankets were
made of natural materials,
including fur, animal skin,
and vegetable fibers.

One artist explained,
"When you make a button
blanket, it takes a long
time. It has to be perfect.
'Good enough' is not
good enough."

Robes of Power

In the beginning, button blankets were made of fur, cedar bark, and tanned skin. The first button blanket crest designs were sewn onto wool blankets acquired from fur traders. By the mid-1800s, button blankets were made of duffle, a very coarse woolen fabric. The weight of the cloth is important. Many dancers do not like the duffle blankets, because they are too heavy. But, if the material is too light, the blanket will not hang or move properly.

The purpose of the button blanket is to show one's crest. Crest designs are **appliquéd,** or cut out and sewn onto a black or dark blue wool blanket. The crest design itself is often cut out of red felt.

A Gift From the Sea

Originally, **abalone** shells were used for buttons. Shining and pearly, they were a treasured gift from the sea. It was believed that the more buttons on a blanket, the more power a person had. One blanket had 1,758 buttons! The firelight danced off the pearly buttons, creating a special effect.

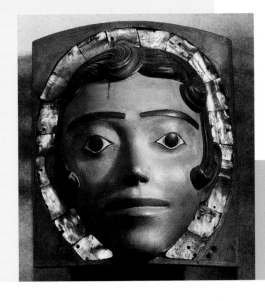

Young Haida women traditionally wear masks when dancing during potlatches or other ceremonies. The borders of the masks are often decorated with abalone shells.

Designing and Sewing a Button Blanket

It takes a great deal of time to design a button blanket. It is more than a design. Just as in the design of totem poles, the meaning of each symbol is very important. Artists use two main shapes in their designs: the ovoid, or oval, and the U-shape.

People who sew button blankets are careful to space the buttons evenly so that the creature will "flow." They think about which parts of the design to emphasize with buttons. There are no buttons along the bottom. This helps the robe to move gracefully when the wearer dances.

Looking to the Future

Many Haida Indians have kept their button blankets carefully stored in wooden boxes for safekeeping. Now, the blankets are being brought out again for special occasions, such as potlatches. People are researching their family names and the crests displayed on the blankets.

Today the Haida people are reclaiming their place in the world through their relationship with the land and through art, dance, and song. There is no word for art in the Haida language. It is simply a part of their culture and who they are. Art has kept the Haida people's spirits alive throughout a long and difficult history. Now, talented Haida artists are passing on their skills in carving and in creating button blankets to another generation. They are helping to continue the rich history of their ancestors.

◄ The objects displayed here, including a button blanket, drum, hat, and pouch, can be seen at potlatches and other Haida ceremonies.

Design Shapes: The Ovoid and U-Shape

Ovoid – It looks like an egg-shape or oval, slightly flattened and concave on the bottom. The bottom corners are sharper than the upper corners. Eyes, heads, and joints are made in the ovoid shape.

U-shape – It looks like a U. It is used for teeth, ears, cheeks, nostrils, tail flukes, and feathers.

Tools

- pencil and eraser
- ruler
- good pair of sewing scissors
- small embroidery scissors
- embroidery needle (#5-8)
- pins
- dressmaker's tracing wheel

Materials

- large piece of white paper
- red felt, 1/2 yd. (1/2 m)
- black or dark blue felt, 1/2 yd. (1/2 m)
- dressmaker's transfer paper
- 50 or more small white 2-hole buttons. You can buy buttons in bulk at fabric stores or thrift stores.
- black and red thread
- dowel (optional)

Planning and sewing this button blanket crest sampler is a good way to learn about traditional design forms of the Haida and other Northwest Coast Indians.

Plan a Crest Sampler

Before you begin to plan your crest, study Haida and other Northwest Coast Indian designs. Look at crests on carvings, prints, totem poles, and button blankets (see Resources, page 46). Read stories about the animals and characters from myths that are pictured in the designs.

Most crest designs belong to specific families. These crests must be earned. It would not be right to copy them. You can design a crest of your very own. It might be a symbol of you, your name, or your family. Can you think of an animal that tells something about your personality? You might want to design a crest for a friend. Button blankets are often made as gifts.

Button blanket robes come in different sizes, but most are about two yards (about 2 m) square. You can learn about button blankets by making a small sampler to hang on your wall.

Make the Pattern

1. Draw a small sketch of your idea. Keep the shapes bold and simple, with no tiny details. Try to include some ovoid and U-shapes in your design (see page 14). Change the shapes to fit the space. One Haida artist believes that if you just keep adding ovoid and U-shapes, you will discover a creature! *(See diagram.)*

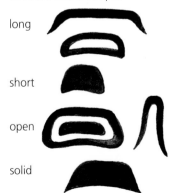

Make the Pattern

1. Ovoid and U-shapes

long

short

open

solid

2. Decide which colors you will use for your crest. A button blanket usually has a background of dark navy blue or black, with a red crest design. Sometimes those colors are reversed. The background might be white or red, with a dark design.

3. Decide on a size and shape for your finished sampler. An 18-inch by 18-inch (46 cm by 46 cm) square is about right. Cut a piece of white paper to the exact size you want your sampler to be. This will be your pattern paper.

15

4. Most blankets have borders on the top and sides to frame the crest. If you want borders, use a ruler to draw them on the pattern paper. Also, draw a center line from top to bottom to help you align the crest. *(See diagram.)*

5. Lightly draw your crest idea on the pattern. Center the design from side to side. Try to fill the space well. *(See diagram.)*

6. Now it's time to make some choices. Some parts of your crest might be solid shapes of felt. Some parts might be thin outlines of felt. Other parts might be outlined with buttons. Carefully draw each part of the design. Draw guidelines on the pattern where you plan to sew the buttons. Adjust the pattern until you are happy with it. *(See diagram.)*

7. Cut out the paper pattern pieces for the crest and the borders. Save the big background pattern piece that you are cutting away.

Sew the Sampler

1. Felt is the best fabric for a small sampler. It doesn't fray, so you won't have to fold the edges under. Spread out the color of felt that you chose for the crest and borders. Pin the paper pattern pieces securely to the felt with pins all around the edges. This will help prevent the pieces from shifting as you cut.

2. Cut around the outside of the pattern pieces. Open the scissors blades wide to cut smoothly. To cut out small inside shapes, first poke a hole in the center of the shape. Use the tip of your small embroidery scissors. *(See diagram.)*

3. Measure and cut the background piece of felt. Arrange all the crest and border pieces on top. You can use the background pattern piece as a guide for placement. Pin the pieces to the background.

◄ Arranging the buttons and crest pieces.

Make the Pattern

4. Draw the borders and center line.

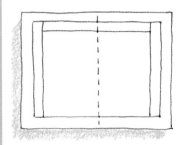

5-6. Draw crest on the pattern.

solid shape

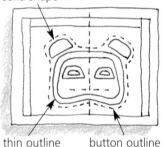

thin outline   button outline

Sew the Sampler

2. Cut the pieces.

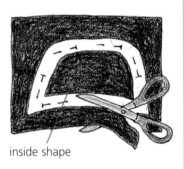

inside shape

4. Sew the crest to the background.

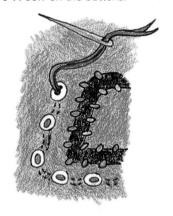

6-7. Sew on the buttons.

4. Sew the crest pieces to the background. Use thread that matches the crest fabric, so the stitches won't show. Use a *tack stitch* or a *running stitch. (See diagram.)*

5. Transfer the button guidelines from the pattern. Use dressmaker's transfer paper, waxy side down, and a tracing wheel. Lay the buttons out on the guidelines. Move them around until you are happy with the placement. Big buttons can be used to emphasize the most important areas of your design.

6. Remove all the buttons from the sampler and lay them in order on the table. Use a double thread to sew on the buttons. From the back of the sampler, sew up through the first button hole. Then, sew back down through the second button hole. *(See diagram.)*

7. Pull the thread tight and go on to the next button. Turn all the button holes so that they line up in a row. Continue sewing down the row of buttons using a *running stitch.* When you reach the end, tie a knot in the thread. You have a finished sampler! *(See diagram.)*

Stitches You Will Use

Thread a needle and tie a knot at the end of the thread. You may use a single or double thread. Start sewing from the back of the background fabric so that the knot will be hidden.

running stitch – Sew in and out of the fabric in a straight line. Make stitches that are even in length.

tack stitch – Take a tiny stitch over the edge of the crest piece. Pull the thread tight. Repeat.

running stitch

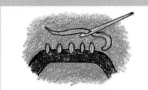

tack stitch

Other Ideas

■ If you want, you can sew loops of felt to the top edge of your sampler. Slide a dowel through the loops to hang it on the wall.

■ Sew shells to your sampler.

■ Add beads for small details.

Carp and Frog samplers ▶
made by students.

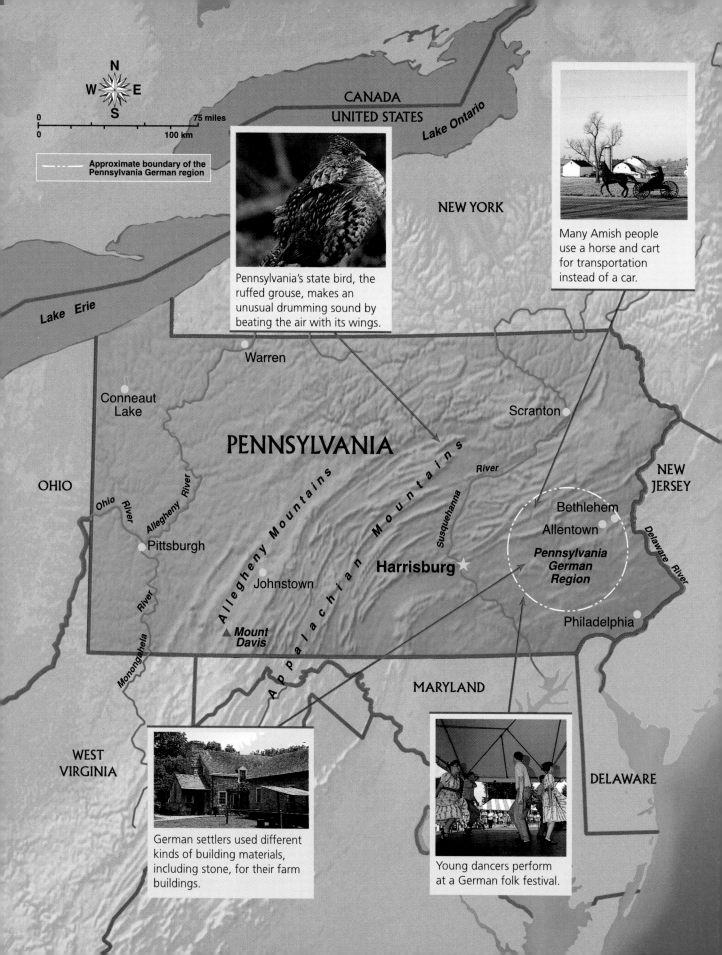

N
W E
S

0 ——————— 75 miles
0 ——————— 100 km

- · - · - Approximate boundary of the
Pennsylvania German region

CANADA
UNITED STATES

Lake Ontario

NEW YORK

Pennsylvania's state bird, the ruffed grouse, makes an unusual drumming sound by beating the air with its wings.

Many Amish people use a horse and cart for transportation instead of a car.

Lake Erie

Warren

Conneaut Lake

Scranton

PENNSYLVANIA

OHIO

River

NEW JERSEY

Ohio River

Allegheny River

Allegheny Mountains

Appalachian Mountains

Susquehanna River

Bethlehem

Allentown

Pennsylvania German Region

Delaware River

Pittsburgh

Johnstown

Harrisburg ★

Philadelphia

River

▲ *Mount Davis*

Appalachian Mountains

MARYLAND

DELAWARE

Monongahela River

WEST VIRGINIA

German settlers used different kinds of building materials, including stone, for their farm buildings.

Young dancers perform at a German folk festival.

Pennsylvania

▲ Pennsylvania's countryside has many beautiful and well-kept farms.

Pennsylvania Facts

Name: Pennsylvania, which means Penn's Woods; "Keystone State" or "Quaker State"
Capital: Harrisburg
Borders: New York, New Jersey, Delaware, Maryland, West Virginia, Ohio, and Lake Erie
Population: 12,056,112
Language: English
Size: 45,302 sq. mi. (117,332 sq km)
High/Low Points: Mt. Davis, 3,213 ft. (979 m); sea level along Delaware River
Rivers/Lakes: Lake Conneaut, Susquehanna River, Delaware River, Ohio River, Allegheny River
Climate: moist climate; average winter temperatures range from above 28° F (-2° C) to below 22° F (-6° C); average July temperatures range from above 74° F (23° C) to below 68° F (20° C)
Wildlife: black bears, ruffed grouse, wild turkeys, fox, otter
Plants: rhododendrons, mountain laurel, wild berries; oak, maple, elm trees

These settlers were often called Pennsylvania Dutch, even though they were actually from Germany. The word *Dutch* probably was a mispronunciation of the German word *Deutsch,* which means "German."

Even barns and covered bridges ▶ were often decorated with hex signs.

The German Settlers Arrive

When the first German settlers arrived in Pennsylvania in 1683, they probably felt right at home. Given their strong agricultural backgrounds, the land before them was a welcome sight. They saw rolling hills, lush farmland, green valleys, and fertile soil. There was a long growing season with plenty of rainfall to grow their crops. The new land was much like the home they had left in the Palatinate region of southwest Germany.

Creating a New Life

The **immigrants** were farmers, but they were also artisans known for their colorful designs and decorations. At first, there was much for them to learn. They had to focus on surviving in a new land. But, after a time, they began to create art again.

They had not been able to bring any of their art with them on the overcrowded ships. They had to create art from memory, using the designs and bright, splashy colors they had used in Germany. Among their first creations were hex signs—large, brightly colored signs placed or painted directly on barns and gates.

Even today, if you drive through southeastern Pennsylvania, you might be lucky enough to spot a barn with hex signs. These signs are vivid examples of Pennsylvania German art and culture.

▲ Amish children sit together at a community meeting.

"Penn's Woods"

The first German settlers came to Pennsylvania by invitation from William Penn. He was an English Quaker who founded Pennsylvania. King Charles II owed Penn's father money. Penn asked for wilderness land in America in payment for the debt. In 1682, he invited a group of German Quakers and people of other faiths to "Penn's Woods." He promised them cheap land and a place to worship freely. These people had all suffered religious **persecution** for years. They wanted a place where they could worship freely without fear of violence.

The journey to America, especially in the early years, was very hard. Many people died. Those who survived faced many challenges in the new land, but they did not complain. Life had been very hard in Germany. They were relieved to escape the endless wars and religious **intolerance,** an unwillingness to accept differences in opinions, including religious beliefs.

In the years that followed, thousands of German families immigrated to Pennsylvania. Until the early 1700s, most immigrants were Quakers, Mennonites, and Amish. They came from Germany, as well as from other countries in Europe. These early settlers were known as the Plain People. They lived in the "old ways" and stood out with their plain, old-fashioned clothing. They followed strict religious principles and opposed formal church practices. In the 1730s, members of the Lutheran and Reformed churches also began to immigrate to Pennsylvania from Germany. They were called "fancy" or "the church people."

William Penn

William Penn was imprisoned several times for his Quaker beliefs. Once, when a jury found Penn "not guilty," the judge threatened to put the jurors in prison unless they changed their verdict. The jurors refused, and they were imprisoned. On appeal, England's highest judges declared that jurors could not be punished for their verdicts. This decision helped to establish the principle of the independence of juries.

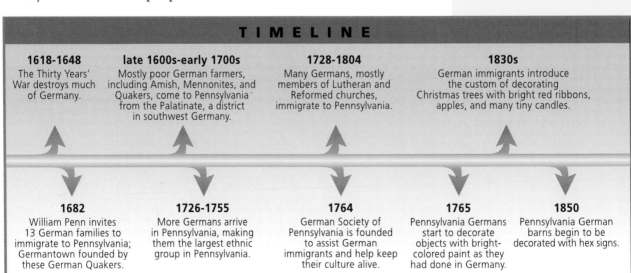

TIMELINE

1618-1648
The Thirty Years' War destroys much of Germany.

late 1600s-early 1700s
Mostly poor German farmers, including Amish, Mennonites, and Quakers, come to Pennsylvania from the Palatinate, a district in southwest Germany.

1728-1804
Many Germans, mostly members of Lutheran and Reformed churches, immigrate to Pennsylvania.

1830s
German immigrants introduce the custom of decorating Christmas trees with bright red ribbons, apples, and many tiny candles.

1682
William Penn invites 13 German families to immigrate to Pennsylvania; Germantown founded by these German Quakers.

1726-1755
More Germans arrive in Pennsylvania, making them the largest ethnic group in Pennsylvania.

1764
German Society of Pennsylvania is founded to assist German immigrants and help keep their culture alive.

1765
Pennsylvania Germans start to decorate objects with bright-colored paint as they had done in Germany.

1850
Pennsylvania German barns begin to be decorated with hex signs.

A New Life

By 1750, Pennsylvania German immigrants made up one-half the population of Pennsylvania. The new settlers were hard-working people whose religious beliefs left little time for entertainment. The Plain People lived in separate communities, spoke no English, and worked hard to retain their own culture.

At first they had no way to show their love of color, because there were no smooth surfaces to paint. There were only crude log houses with rough surfaces. When buildings and furniture started to be made with smooth wood, they could think about decorating them.

▲ German painters create beautiful designs on a variety of surfaces.

Pennsylvania German Barns

The Pennsylvania Germans were gifted farmers. They built very large barns to house their animals and hay. Whenever possible, the barns were built on slopes. This allowed a hay wagon to be driven directly into the upper story. The animals were housed below. In the early days, the barns were made from rough logs with thatched roofs. Later, they were made of stone and smooth wood.

Around 1765, the settlers' art began to come to life. Bright red paint was not expensive, and they used it on every smooth surface they could find. They painted their large barns bright red, a custom that set them apart from other settlers. Some neighbors were critical, noting that everything seemed to be coated with red. The broad wooden sides of the barns were sometimes 100 feet (30 m) long. These large surfaces were perfect for the colorful, large, round hex signs that began to appear around 1850.

The bright red barns were a bold advertisement for the Pennsylvania Germans' successful farming practices that included **crop rotation** and returning natural elements to the soil.

Visitors to the Pennsylvania ▶ German region can take a tour of barns and other buildings that display hex signs.

Hex signs often have flowers, hearts, sunbursts, and other designs.

Hex Signs

Hex signs first appeared in Europe in the Middle Ages. At first, they had a definite religious importance. There is disagreement about the purpose of the hex signs painted on Pennsylvania German barns. Some people believe the signs protected barns and livestock from lightning and evil spirits, or prevented milk from turning sour. However, most people believe the purpose was just for decoration.

Most hex signs are round with designs that have four, six, or eight divisions. Six divisions were most common, because they were easy to make using a large wooden compass and straight edge. They can be five to six feet (1.5 to 2 m) across. Smaller hex signs are painted on round panels and are hung on gates and houses. Geometric designs, such as sunbursts and stars, are often used, along with daisies, tulips, and hearts. The *distelfink* (goldfinch), a good-luck symbol, is also found in many hex designs.

The Pennsylvania Germans used many bright colors in their hex signs. Red, yellow, green, blue, and white were used most often. These colors stood out against the broad red background of the barns they decorated.

Tourism and "Progress"

Tourism and "progress" make it increasingly difficult for the Plain People to maintain their special way of life. Malls and clusters of houses now dot the rural Pennsylvania landscape. Many hex signs have been painted over instead of being repainted. In another one hundred years, will hex signs be seen only in books and in museums? Only time will tell if the descendants of the original Pennsylvania German immigrant families will be able to preserve their ancestors' beliefs and traditions.

Meaning of Color to the Pennsylvania Germans	
red	emotions, creativity
yellow	love of people, the sun
green	growth of plants and ideas
blue	protection, peace
white	purity, the moon
brown	mother earth, friendship

The multicolored *distelfink* is used in many Pennsylvania German designs. It is a symbol of good luck and happiness. Legend has it that when God painted the birds, the *distelfink* was last, so God used all the leftover paints to color it.

Tools

- very sharp pencil
- ruler
- scissors
- smooth, flat board, such as a drafting board
- compass that opens at least 6 in. (15 cm) wide (A beam compass that slides on a rod is best for making large circles. You can try a pencil tied to a string with a pin at one end. The pin marks the center of the circle you will draw.)
- protractor
- colored markers
- paintbrushes (a flat brush and a thin, round brush)

Materials

- tape
- paper
- piece of thin plywood or hardboard 12 in. (30 cm) or larger; cut into a circle if desired
- sandpaper
- white latex enamel paint
- transfer paper
- acrylic paints (available in art and craft stores)
- polyurethane sealer (optional)

Designing a hex sign is a fun way to learn about circles, stars, and other shapes.

Tools

compass

beam compass

protractor

Experiment with Hex Designs

Hex signs are round and **symmetrical.** They have matching parts that radiate out from the center. You'll use a compass, protractor, and ruler to draw them. They require careful measuring and a sharp point on your pencil. Draw on a smooth board so your lines will be crisp and the compass point will have a surface to sink into.

1. Before starting your hex sign, practice drawing a few different designs. Cut several pieces of white paper to 8 1/2 inches by 8 1/2 inches (22 cm by 22 cm). Fold them each in quarters to find the center point. Unfold and tape one piece to the board.

2. Open the compass to 4 inches (10 cm). This will be the *radius* of your circle. The radius is the distance from the center of the circle to the outside edge. Tighten the screw on the compass, so that the compass won't slip as you use it.

3. Put the pointed part of the compass on the center point of the paper. Hold the compass down firmly. Draw the *circumference,* or outside edge, of the circle. *(See diagram.)*

Students use compasses and protractors
▼ to draw their hex signs.

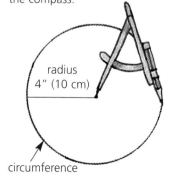

Experiment with Hex Designs

3. Draw the circle with the compass.

radius
4" (10 cm)

circumference

Star Designs

5 pointed star
10 sections
36 degrees apart

6 pointed star
12 sections
30 degrees apart

8 pointed star
16 sections
22.5 degrees apart

Star Design

1. To make a star design, divide the circle into even sections. Measure the sections by *degrees,* the units of measure for a circle. Each star design uses a different number of sections. Each combination of sections will add up to 360 degrees, or a whole circle.

2. Use a protractor to measure the sections. Line up the bottom center of the protractor with the center point of your circle. Mark the sections carefully with a pencil. Mark one side of the circle. Then rotate the protractor and mark the other side. *(See diagram.)*

3. Using a ruler, draw a straight line from one edge of the circle to the other. Draw through two section marks and the center point. This line is the *diameter* of the circle. Continue to draw diameter lines until all the section marks are connected. The circle will look like a wheel with spokes. Put a colored dot on the circumference at the end of *every other spoke. (See diagram.)*

4. Use the compass to make a smaller inner circle. Find the ends of the spokes without colored dots. Make dots on these spokes where they meet the circumference of the inner circle. Use a ruler to draw straight lines from the outer dots to the inner dots. You have a star! *(See diagram.)*

Flower Design

1. Tape down a new piece of paper on your board. Draw a circle with a 4-inch (10 cm) radius. Keep the compass open to the size of the radius. Put the point of the compass at any spot on the circumference. Draw a wide curve with your compass from the circumference, through the center, and back to the circumference. *(See diagram.)*

2. Move the point of the compass to one end of the first curve, where it touches the circumference of the circle. Draw another curve. Continue to draw curves until at least six petals are formed. *(See diagram.)*

Star Design

2. Use a protractor to measure the sections.

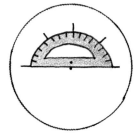

3. Draw diameter lines across the circle.

colored dots

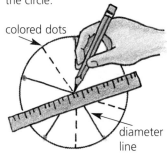

diameter line

4. Make an inner circle. Connect the dots.

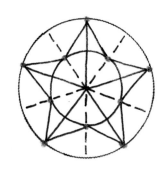

Flower Design

1-2. Draw a flower design.

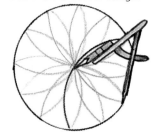

Design Ideas

■ Divide and paint the rays of a star in contrasting colors so they appear to swirl.

■ Draw one design to fill a circle inside of another design.

■ Design a border around the outside edge.

■ Add other images between the petals or star points. Think of a symbol that gives you a feeling of good luck.

Make a Pattern

Now that you've practiced some basic designs, you are ready to plan your hex sign. You can vary the basic designs in many ways. Look at the ideas on the left.

1. Make a rough drawing of your ideas, and plan the colors. Use bright colors with a strong contrast. Decide how big you will make your hex sign. A good size is between 12 and 18 inches (30 and 45 cm) in diameter.

2. Make the pattern. Cut a square of white paper a little larger than the finished hex sign. Fold the paper in quarters to find the center point. Open the paper again and tape it to the board.

3. Open the compass to the radius (half of the diameter) of your hex sign. Draw the circumference. To make a border, close the legs of your compass 1/2 inch (1 cm) or more. Draw another circle a little smaller than the first.

4. Draw your star or flower as planned. Use the protractor to mark the placement of any other images. Draw these and you are done.

Paint Your Hex Sign

1. Sand the board you will use for your hex sign. Paint it with two base coats of white paint. **When painting, protect your clothing with an old shirt or a smock. When wet, acrylic paint can be removed with water. After it dries, it cannot be removed.** Allow the board to dry completely.

2. Place a piece of transfer paper (waxy side down) on the board. Tape your paper pattern on top. Trace over the design with a ballpoint pen.

3. Mix the colors you plan to use. Paint one color at a time. Take your time, and let each section dry before you paint the next. Use the flat brush for open areas and the thin brush for the lines.

4. Let the paint dry overnight. Acrylic paint is fast-drying. Seal the finished hex sign with polyurethane if you want.

Students' hex signs.

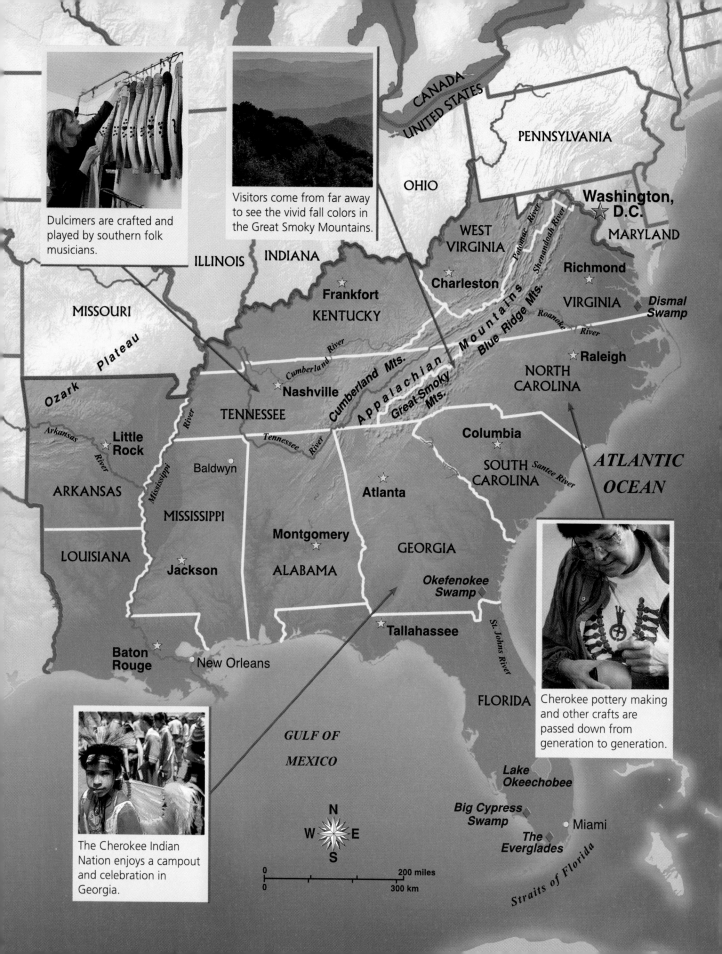

Dulcimers are crafted and played by southern folk musicians.

Visitors come from far away to see the vivid fall colors in the Great Smoky Mountains.

CANADA
UNITED STATES

PENNSYLVANIA

OHIO

Washington, D.C.

MARYLAND

WEST VIRGINIA

Charleston

Richmond

VIRGINIA

Dismal Swamp

Potomac River

Shenandoah River

ILLINOIS   INDIANA

Frankfort

KENTUCKY

Cumberland River

Appalachian Mountains

Cumberland Mts.

Blue Ridge Mts.

Roanoke River

Raleigh

NORTH CAROLINA

MISSOURI

Plateau

Nashville

TENNESSEE

Great Smoky Mts.

Ozark

Arkansas River

Little Rock

Mississippi River

Baldwyn

Tennessee River

Columbia

SOUTH CAROLINA

Santee River

ATLANTIC OCEAN

ARKANSAS

MISSISSIPPI

Atlanta

LOUISIANA

Montgomery

GEORGIA

Jackson

ALABAMA

Okefenokee Swamp

St. Johns River

Baton Rouge

New Orleans

Tallahassee

FLORIDA

GULF OF MEXICO

Cherokee pottery making and other crafts are passed down from generation to generation.

The Cherokee Indian Nation enjoys a campout and celebration in Georgia.

N
W   E
S

0   200 miles
0   300 km

Lake Okeechobee

Big Cypress Swamp

Miami

The Everglades

Straits of Florida

Southern United States

Folk Arts in the Southern United States

Driving from Florida to North Carolina, it is possible to find hundreds of folk art shops, festivals, and workshops. One might visit the Mossy Creek Barnyard Arts and Crafts Festival in Georgia, Tennessee's Black Folklife Festival, Kentucky's Appalachian Celebration, and the Cherokee Fall Festival in North Carolina.

The South's rich folk art tradition was influenced by three distinct cultures: Native Americans, African Americans, and European settlers. These groups adapted to the land and to living near to each other. Each group had its own crafts and was influenced by the crafts of the other groups. Artisans took advantage of the area's rich natural materials, such as reeds and wood. They used hand tools to create quilts, baskets, toys, brooms, weavings, and woodcarvings.

The History of Southern Woodcarving

Many varieties of trees grew in the lush Southern forests. Because wood was plentiful, early settlers used wood instead of iron to make many things they needed to survive. Bowls, spoons, furniture, wheels, and wagons were all made of wood. They also made birdhouses, musical instruments, boats, toys, and walking canes. Southern woodworkers learned to identify the differences in color, grain, and hardness of each type of tree. Today, two groups of people in the South, African Americans and the Eastern Band of the Cherokee Indians, continue these rich woodcarving traditions.

◀ Cherokee artisans create a variety of beautiful weavings, baskets, woodcarvings, and masks.

African American ▶ woodcarver Arthur Dilbert begins his carving by cutting down a large piece of wood.

Cherokee Woodcarving

The Eastern Band of the Cherokee Indians in North Carolina have carved and **whittled** wood for hundreds of years. In earlier times, they carved utensils for cooking. They also made toys for children. Today, they carve beautiful animal figures out of smooth-grained buckeye, walnut, and wild cherry trees found on their reservation in western North Carolina. The Cherokee carvers operate an Arts and Crafts Cooperative. The cooperative supports them in selling their works and teaching their craft to others.

▲ Cherokee woodcarver Virgil Ledford calls this work "The Eagle Capture."

Cherokee Wooden Masks

Carved, painted, and decorated wood represented the spirit world to southern Native American and African American groups. Today, the tradition of carving masks is still practiced by a small number of Cherokee men. These wooden **decoy** masks are carved to look like bear, buffalo, and other wildlife. In the past, hunters wore these masks during ceremonial dances to ensure a good hunt. They also used them to avoid being noticed when sneaking up on an animal.

▲ Eastern Cherokee tribal elder Walter Calhoun displays a traditional carved mask with help from his grandson.

The Cherokee rattlesnake mask is a human face with a rattlesnake curled on top of the head. Medicine men used the mask to help cure illness. A Cherokee warrior wore this mask to let people know he intended to fight. Other masks often carved by Cherokee maskmakers represented white settlers, African Americans, and other Indian tribes who threatened the Cherokee people. They were used in ceremonial dances to keep intruders out of their area.

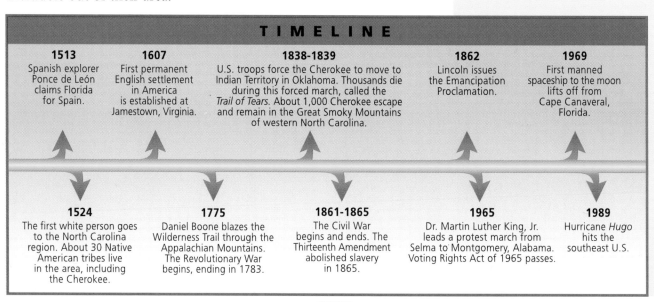

TIMELINE

1513
Spanish explorer Ponce de León claims Florida for Spain.

1607
First permanent English settlement in America is established at Jamestown, Virginia.

1838-1839
U.S. troops force the Cherokee to move to Indian Territory in Oklahoma. Thousands die during this forced march, called the *Trail of Tears*. About 1,000 Cherokee escape and remain in the Great Smoky Mountains of western North Carolina.

1862
Lincoln issues the Emancipation Proclamation.

1969
First manned spaceship to the moon lifts off from Cape Canaveral, Florida.

1524
The first white person goes to the North Carolina region. About 30 Native American tribes live in the area, including the Cherokee.

1775
Daniel Boone blazes the Wilderness Trail through the Appalachian Mountains. The Revolutionary War begins, ending in 1783.

1861-1865
The Civil War begins and ends. The Thirteenth Amendment abolished slavery in 1865.

1965
Dr. Martin Luther King, Jr. leads a protest march from Selma to Montgomery, Alabama. Voting Rights Act of 1965 passes.

1989
Hurricane *Hugo* hits the southeast U.S.

African American Woodcarving Traditions

Woodcarving is one of the earliest art forms with strong roots in Africa. Ancient carvings have been found in dry areas in Africa that date back thousands of years. The carving of wooden masks and small statues was common to many African tribes. It was also a tradition in Africa for holy men to carve **conjuring** canes. They tossed these canes into the air to get the attention of the gods. Today, African American woodcarvers in the South create walking canes.

Walking Canes

African American woodcarvers draw from their African heritage and their history in the South to create unique walking canes, or walking sticks. The walking canes are usually carved from hardwoods, such as oak, dogwood, and sourwood trees. Using hardwoods makes the canes strong. Carvers may make canes for themselves or create one especially for a buyer. The cane and its carved handle must fit the owner's height and hand in order to work well. Each walking stick contains symbols with personal meaning for the owner.

Many canes feature carvings of powerful animals and reptiles. Snakes, lizards, turtles, alligators, lions, and eagles are often used. Human faces or the human figure are also used. The woodcarver may carve a symbol into the stick that relates to the owner's occupation. A carpenter's cane may have a hammer on it. A train may be carved into a railroad worker's cane.

Elijah Pierce

Famous African American woodcarver and barber Elijah Pierce was born in Baldwyn, Mississippi, in 1892. In his mid-sixties, he began carving the story of his life into an elaborate walking stick. The project took him 20 years. Pierce's walking stick contains symbols from his family history, stories from the Bible, and images from his life. Pierce carved combs, a barber's chair, a cross, and even words to stories he wanted to remember into the cane. He was often asked to preach in his local church. He would turn his cane over and over until he found a story or message he wanted to use. He called his walking stick his "preaching stick."

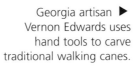
Georgia artisan ▶ Vernon Edwards uses hand tools to carve traditional walking canes.

◀ Artisans carve beautiful walking cane handles inspired by powerful animals and human features and activities.

Wood Spirits

In both Africa and in the South, there is a practice of placing wood on graves. A tree is believed to be a sign of the spirit on its way to the other world. Many African American woodcarvers and sculptors believe that there is a spirit in the wood. The artist's job is to select, carve, and decorate a piece of wood to reveal the unique spirit or creature within it.

Often wood sculptures created by African American folk artists are **abstract.** They do not represent real animal or human forms that are easily recognized. Instead, they are powerful images that offer a number of possibilities. In most African American folk art forms, no two works are the same. Each creation represents the artist's skill and vision.

▲ This detailed buffalo woodcarving shows the animal's size and strength, even though the work itself is small.

Sculpting Wood Spirits

Some wood artists carve *into* the wood, reducing it until the figure inside begins to form. They would be offended if someone asked them to "make a horse." Instead, the carver would sense if a horse was in the wood. If so, he would carve until the image appeared. As one carver said, "Don't ask me to carve something particular out of a piece of wood. It might not be there."

When some carvers see the creature or character in a piece of wood, they add to it to bring out the figure inside. They decorate it with pieces of wood, paint, photos, magazine pictures, hair, glitter, or other objects. This approach allows the artist to create a figure of a creature or person that draws out the spirit inside the wood.

▲ This carving of famous African American Frederick Douglass was created by Vernon Edwards.

◄ These playful carvings were created by Cherokee members of the Qualla Arts and Crafts Mutual.

Tools

- wire brush
- small pruning clippers
- small handsaw
- wood rasp
- C-clamps
- hand drill, or a brace and bits
- hammer
- crescent wrench or wrench set
- paintbrushes

Materials

- 2-3 pieces of weathered wood (driftwood, branches, tree roots, sticks, twigs, pieces of bark, lumber scraps)
- other small objects (rocks, shells, nuts, corks, fabric scraps, feathers, yarn, beads)
- sandpaper
- carpenter's wood glue
- masking tape
- wire or strong string
- nails and lag screws (with hex-shaped heads)
- acrylic paints
- wax furniture polish or linseed oil

Your sculpture will be made of wood scraps and other materials you have collected. The creation of each creature will be an interesting challenge.

Woodworking Tools

wire brush

clippers

wood rasp

brace and bits

crescent wrench

hand drill

Woodworking Safety

- You must have an adult work with you.
- Learn the correct way to use a tool, and use it for its intended purpose only.
- Use common sense! Cut away from yourself and others.
- Do not force or jam the tool into the wood. Let the tool do the work.
- Always clamp the wood to a stable base before sawing or drilling.
- Put tools away when you are finished with them.

Gather the Materials

Finding the materials for your sculpture is half the fun. Go for a walk in a park. Take a trip to a river, lake, or ocean shore to look for driftwood. Go for a hike in the woods and gather interesting sticks, bark, and old tree roots. Stay home and poke around in your own backyard for scraps of weathered lumber or pruned limbs. Don't collect any wood that is rotten and falling apart.

Keep your eyes open for any piece of wood that looks unusual. Weathered wood has beautiful colors, shapes, and textures. A twisted branch may already look like a strange creature. As you begin looking, you'll see possibilities everywhere!

Clean the wood as soon as you get it home. Remove dirt by rubbing the wood with a wire brush. Then soak the wood in a bucket of water overnight. This will force out insects that may be hiding in the cracks. Allow the wood to dry in an airy spot.

Make a Creature

You will bring your creature to life step by step. Go slowly. Each piece of wood will need a different approach. Only experience will help you decide which method to use. Whenever you're uncertain, experiment with a scrap of wood first. Be sure to follow the woodworking safety tips on page 31, and let an adult work closely with you.

1. Pick out the piece of wood from your collection that interests you the most. Set it on a table and examine it. Turn it in several directions. What does it remind you of? Get a sense of the wood's spirit, or character. Is it graceful, comical, or strange in some way? Does the wood resemble a creature, real or imaginary? Begin to create a picture in your mind of the creature and its personality.

2. Now, decide how your creature will stand. It can balance on three or more legs, or rest on a flat edge. Your piece of wood may have twigs and branches that will work as legs. Use clippers to remove extra branches and shorten any legs that are too long. Work slowly. Take off a little bit at a time. It's easy to remove a branch but much harder to put it back! *(See diagram.)*

3. Sometimes you may have thicker parts of wood to remove. **If so, ask an adult to remove them with a handsaw.** *(See diagram.)*

4. If your creature is not yet stable, you'll need to add a leg or two. Look through your collection of sticks and wood scraps to find the perfect piece. **Ask an adult to help you trim the new leg to the proper length with clippers or a handsaw.** Use a rasp to shape the top of the leg so it fits firmly against the body. Create as large a surface for contact as possible between the two objects.

5. There are many ways to join the new leg to your creature's body. You can attach a small leg with carpenter's wood glue. Apply glue to both surfaces and line up the parts. Use a clamp or masking tape to hold the pieces together while they dry. Wait 30 minutes before you remove the clamp or tape. *(See diagram.)*

◄ Students begin to bring creatures to life.

Make a Creature

2. Shorten and remove branches.

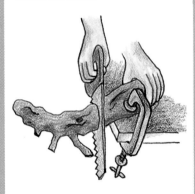

3. An adult can remove thicker parts of the wood with a handsaw.

5. Join the new leg.

Make a Creature

6. Join a larger leg.

reinforce with string or wire

drill a hole

▲ This lag screw makes a long neck.

Other Ideas

■ Try connecting parts of your creature so that they wiggle or turn. How about attaching a head with a large spring?

■ Drill a hole in an arm. Fasten it with a thin nail so that it spins.

6. For a larger size leg, glue may not be enough. Use strong string or wire to make the joint strong. Sometimes it works best to drill a hole that the leg can be plugged into. This allows for more surface contact with the glue. *(See diagram.)*

7. Nails or screws work well in some cases. Use a hand drill to make a starting hole. Drill a hole that's a little smaller than the diameter of the screw or nail. Lag screws are easy to insert. They turn in with a crescent wrench instead of a screwdriver.

8. When your creature is stable, stop and look it over again. You can begin to add other wood pieces. Perhaps it needs a head, wings, or a tail. Ask yourself if an addition is the right one for your creature. Attach one body part at a time, and let the glue dry thoroughly.

9. When the main body parts are attached, you're ready to finish the wood surface. What do you want the skin of your creature to look like? You can leave rough bark and bits of lichen growing on it, or you can sand it smooth.

10. Add linseed oil to darken and protect the wood. Or, paint the surface with designs and patterns. **When painting, protect your clothing with an old shirt or a smock. When wet, acrylic paint can be removed with water. After it dries, it cannot be removed.**

11. Now it's time to add details! Look through the odds and ends you have collected. Pick out items that fit the character of your creature. Paint the eyes, carve them out, or glue on pebbles or beads. How about leather scraps for ears, a shell for a nose, and lichen for a beard? You could use ribbons for stripes and thumbtacks for spots. Anything goes, as long as it fits the spirit of your creature.

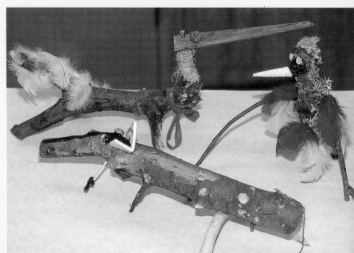

Three ▶ finished wood creatures.

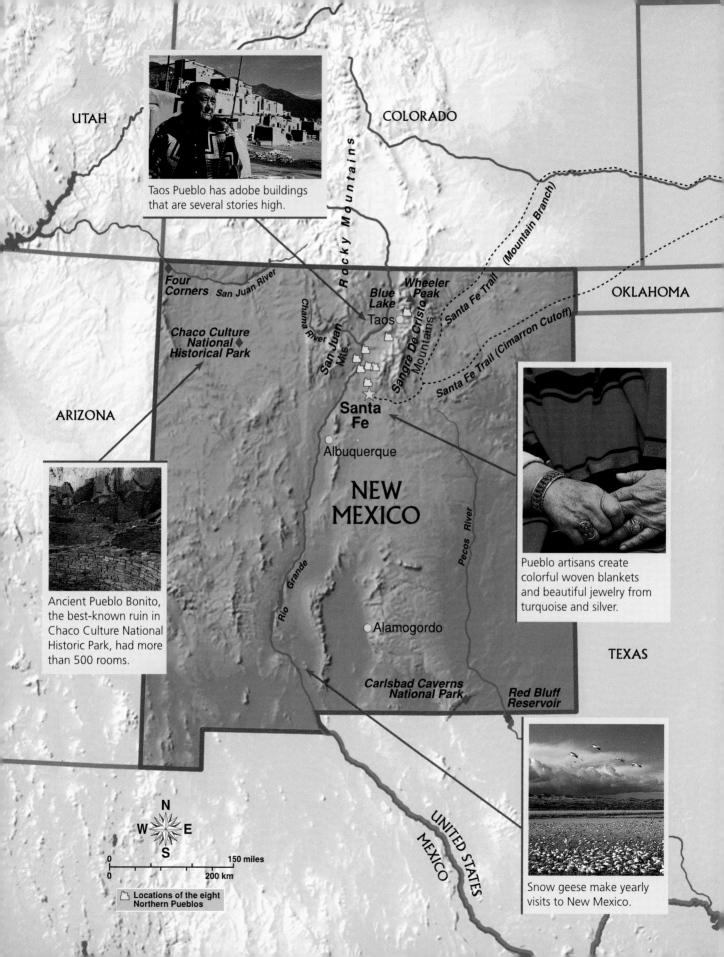

UTAH

COLORADO

Taos Pueblo has adobe buildings that are several stories high.

Four Corners

San Juan River

Chaco Culture National Historical Park

ARIZONA

Chama River

San Juan Mts

Rocky Mountains

Blue Lake

Wheeler Peak

Taos

Sangre De Cristo Mountains

Santa Fe Trail

(Mountain Branch)

OKLAHOMA

Santa Fe Trail (Cimarron Cutoff)

Santa Fe

Albuquerque

NEW MEXICO

Pecos River

Pueblo artisans create colorful woven blankets and beautiful jewelry from turquoise and silver.

TEXAS

Ancient Pueblo Bonito, the best-known ruin in Chaco Culture National Historic Park, had more than 500 rooms.

Rio Grande

Alamogordo

Carlsbad Caverns National Park

Red Bluff Reservoir

UNITED STATES

MEXICO

N
W E
S

0   150 miles
0   200 km

Locations of the eight Northern Pueblos

Snow geese make yearly visits to New Mexico.

New Mexico

Arts of the Northern Pueblos

Every July, artisans of the eight northern pueblos of New Mexico hold the Artist and Craftsman Show. It celebrates the arts, dances, foods, and music of the Pueblo culture. It is a source of great pride for the Pueblo people. Only work that is handmade in the traditional way is displayed and sold. Pueblo children who are learning crafts have their own area to exhibit their work. It's a chance for visitors to see Native American culture as it has been practiced for centuries.

There are 19 Native American pueblos in New Mexico. Each one preserves the traditions and customs practiced by its ancestors. Among these cherished traditions is the art of handcrafted coil pottery.

The Land of Enchantment

New Mexico's enchantment lies in the beauty of its landscape. But the story of its many peoples is equally fascinating. The ancient Native Americans were joined by two other groups of people. Descendants of Spanish explorers and settlers bring a rich Hispanic culture to the state. During pioneer days, the Santa Fe Trail brought many Easterners and European prospectors, miners, railroad workers, and shopkeepers. At the Artist and Craftsman Show, people from all backgrounds enjoy hundreds of booths celebrating Pueblo art and culture.

A Showcase of Pueblo Art and Culture

"If you come with a respectful outlook and an open heart, you may leave with more than a pretty pot and a full stomach. You may leave with a sense of the harmony that the Pueblo People, with their ancient connection to the earth, bring to us all."

Eight Northern Indian Pueblo Council

▲ Pueblo children perform the Buffalo Dance at tribal ceremonies.

▲ The Chama River flows through land that is alive with the colors of New Mexico.

A Land of Many Colors and Shapes

New Mexico's landscape is as varied as its people. It looks as if an artist has been at work with an enormous palette of colors. Under a brilliant blue sky, red rock mesas and white, snow-capped mountains tower over dry sandy deserts. Rivers filled with deep red clay flow through narrow rock canyons. Cool green forests surround sparkling blue mountain lakes. Isolated hills or mountains, called mesas or buttes, are painted in bands of bright red, yellow, purple, and grayish blue. Black lava rock from extinct volcanoes covers large areas.

New Mexico is also a land of unusual shapes. Colorful rock formations look like fortresses, castles, unearthly beings, and arched bridges. The bent and twisted trees in its **petrified** forests and the shapes of desert cacti add to New Mexico's haunting appearance. Carlsbad Caverns is one of the largest cave systems in the world. It has huge vaulted rooms with enormous **stalagmite** statues and **stalactite** "icicles" hanging down.

Many artists have been drawn to New Mexico because of its unique colors, shapes, and light. For centuries, Native American artists have used materials from the land to create pottery that reflects the state's rich colors and designs.

The Four Corners

New Mexico's northwest corner meets the borders of Arizona, Utah, and Colorado. It is the only place in the United States where four states meet.

The white and pastel ▶ colored stalactites and stalagmites in Carlsbad Caverns form icicles, pillars, and other mysterious shapes. Carlsbad Caverns became a national park in 1930.

The Ancient Ones

Native American people lived in New Mexico thousands of years ago. The "outsiders who vanished" are called the Anasazi. They believed that they came into this world through a hole in the earth. The Anasazi were tied to the earth with devotion and respect. Their cliff dwellings, art forms, ceremonies, and dances all speak to the importance of living in harmony with the earth that gave them life. The Pueblo are descendants of the Anasazi.

▲ Petroglyphs, or stone paintings, created by the ancient Anasazi people tell of the arrival of Spanish horsemen.

Spanish Explorers

Francisco Coronado was the first Spanish explorer to enter the area in 1540, looking for gold. He used *pueblo*, the Spanish word for city, to describe the villages shining in the sunset. The Spanish conquerors left a trail of destruction and terror. They demanded that the Pueblo people give up their religion and convert to Christianity. When the people did not obey, they were imprisoned, enslaved, tortured, and killed.

The San Juan Revolt

In 1680, the Pueblo people united and overthrew the Spanish. This bloody uprising forced the Spanish to leave New Mexico for 12 years. In the San Juan Pueblo, a medicine man named Popé organized all Pueblo leaders into a military attack against the Spanish. Popé planned the attack so each pueblo revolted on the same day. The battle lasted for nine days. In the end, Spanish officials, priests, and settlers fled the area in defeat.

When the Spanish returned and reconquered the area in 1692, they treated the Pueblo people more fairly. They recognized that the Native American and Christian religions had to exist side by side. As New Mexico developed and finally became part of the United States, this respect for differences has resulted in a rich cultural society.

TIMELINE

A.D. 1 - 1300	1680	1692	1846	1912	1970
Anasazi Indians live in northwestern New Mexico.	Popé leads the Pueblo Revolt.	The Spanish regain control.	The Mexican War breaks out.	New Mexico becomes a state.	Congress recognizes the Taos Pueblo claim to its sacred Blue Lake.

1540-1542	1598	1821	1850	1945
Coronado explores the Southwest.	First Spanish settlement in New Mexico, San Juan de Los Caballeros, established near Chama River.	Mexico wins independence from Spain; the Santa Fe trail opens.	New Mexico becomes a U.S. territory.	Atom bomb testing on July 16 at Alamogordo.

San Juan Pueblo

San Juan Pueblo is located where two rivers, the Rio Grande and Rio Chama, join. With about 2,000 tribal members, it is the largest of the six Tewa-speaking villages. To its people, it is known as *Ohkay Owingeh*, which means "strong people." It is considered the "mother village" of the Tewa people.

Houses in San Juan Pueblo are connected, much like apartment buildings. They are made out of stone or **adobe** bricks and plastered with mud. Ceremonial dances are held in the plaza, or central square. San Juan, like most other pueblos, has a **kiva** chamber. Religious ceremonies and gatherings are held in the kiva. The San Juan Pueblo also has a Catholic church, its own government, police department, community school, and office of education.

San Juan's people work to keep their tribal arts and traditions alive. They have formed businesses that guide the business of the pueblo and support traditional crafts, like pottery. The pueblo also supports a growing herd of buffalo. The people have started a Buffalo Project to restore the Tewa people's spiritual connection to the buffalo.

Living in Harmony

Religion is very important to the Pueblo people. They do not separate religion from everyday life. They believe that all people must live in harmony with the universe. One way to maintain harmony is to perform ceremonies throughout the year. Dances serve as prayers for rain, plentiful harvests, and the well-being of all.

◀ Ceremonies and dances help keep Pueblo beliefs and culture alive.

Ceremonies and Festivals in San Juan Pueblo

January	Cloud Dance Transfer of Canes King's Day
February	Deer Dance
June	Saint Anthony's Feast Day San Juan Pueblo Feast Day
August	Pueblo Revolt Day
September	Harvest Dance
December	Matachine or Ritual Dance Turtle Dance

Pueblo Pottery

In New Mexico, the art of making pottery is almost 2,000 years old. As in other pueblos, San Juan Pueblo's coiled pottery served as cooking pots, vessels for ceremonies, and storage jars for water and grain. Today, people in every pueblo know how to make the traditional pottery.

Each pueblo has its own place to dig clay. It comes in many natural colors, including reds, browns, grays, and even a pure white. When clay comes from the ground, it is very hard. Potters soak it in water and grind it until it becomes soft enough to work by hand. Fine sand, powdered shells, or crushed sandstone are worked into the clay to make it stronger. Then it will not crack during firing, or baking.

Pottery Designs

The color of the clay, firing methods, and the potter's designs make each pueblo's pottery different from that of other pueblos.

San Juan Pueblo potters make several different types of pots. One type is a polished, solid red pot, with or without a design. San Juan Pueblo potters also create light brown pots. These pots may have a design carved into the surface.

Many Pueblo crafts, including pottery, have been changed by new ideas, tools, materials, and markets. Today, Pueblo pottery is considered a work of art. Potters now make smaller, more decorative pieces for purchase by art collectors and tourists. Many potters make a living by selling their work.

▲ Santa Clara Pueblo is famous for its red pottery.

▲ San Ildefonso Pueblo potter Elvis Torres paints a water serpent design.

▲ San Juan Pueblo potter Diego Aguino creates pottery with carefully etched designs.

Mother Earth

For centuries, Pueblo potters have believed that Mother Earth has a spirit. Her permission must be asked before clay can be dug from her. People believed that sickness would result if clay was gathered without the correct ceremony.

▲ Santa Clara Pueblo potter Tina Garcia takes her time as she builds a coil pot.

Coiled Pottery

Pueblo potters do not use a potter's wheel. Potters use their fingers to press small pots into a shape. They build larger pots with coils. Potters roll long ropes of clay and coil them into a desired shape. They pinch the coils together and scrape the pot smooth with a piece of gourd to wipe out any sign of the coil ridges. Potters apply slip, a mixture of water and very fine clay, to the pot. They polish it with a small, smooth stone. Designs are painted using brushes often made from **yucca** stems.

After the pot dries, it is fired or baked in an earth pit. In some pueblos, potters use cakes of cow manure for fuel, because it gives an even heat. Others use hot coals or wood instead. The firing takes several hours. The firing method can affect the pot's color.

▲ Pueblo potters often use stems from the yucca plant as brushes to paint their designs.

Maria Martinez 1887–1980

As a child in the San Ildefonso Pueblo, Maria Martinez learned the art of coiled pottery from older women in her family. She is one of the greatest Native American artists who ever lived. Maria and her husband, Julian, brought world attention to the ancient art of Pueblo pottery. In 1907, Julian was working with visiting archaeologists who dug up some ancient Anasazi pots. At the archaeologists' request, Maria and Julian went to work making similar pots. In the process they discovered the technique for creating a black matte design against a polished black design. In the beginning they sold their pots for as little as five dollars. Today their work is so valuable that it is considered priceless.

Tools

- small board to work on
- plastic or linen cloth
- smock, apron, or an old shirt
- clay needle tool and loop tool
- scraper (wooden modeling tool, spoon handle, or an ice-cream stick)
- small piece of nylon window screen
- sponge
- dust mask
- 2-cup (1/2-liter) measuring cup
- small plastic containers with lids
- smooth stones and agates of different sizes
- paintbrushes
- access to a low-fire kiln (cone 06)

Materials

- a chunk of white low-fire clay with grog (crushed pottery) or sand added; available in art supply stores
- ceramic stains, terra-cotta and cobalt-free black, 1 oz. (28 grams) each; available at art supply stores, or see Resources on page 47 for ordering information

Pottery making takes concentration. Give yourself plenty of time, so you can enjoy the process without feeling rushed.

Clay Tools

needle tool

loop tool

scraper (modeling tool)

Clay Safety

Dry clay creates dust that is very bad for your lungs. To protect yourself, remember to do these things:

- Clean your worktable with a wet sponge before the clay dries.
- Cover your clothes with a smock. Wash the smock when you are finished working.
- Wear a dust mask when you are sanding or smoothing dry clay.

Prepare the Clay

Purchase clay with grog or sand added. These make the clay stronger and less sticky, which works best for hand building.

1. You will need a small board for your work surface. Cover the board with a plastic or linen cloth, and tape down the edges. This will keep the clay from sticking. Put the board on a very solid table or on the ground.

2. Next, prepare the clay. Remove air bubbles by throwing the clay forcefully onto the board about ten times. Air bubbles can cause the pot to explode in the kiln.

3. The clay should be easy to mold but not sticky. If the clay is sticky, leave it on the board to dry a bit. Otherwise, cover the prepared clay with plastic until you need to use it.

Make a Pot

Pueblo potters do not plan their pots. They let the clay take on or form the shape it wants. Your first coil pot may turn out a little lopsided and uneven. Allow yourself to experiment and have fun. When you are finished, you can decide whether to keep the pot or flatten it and start over.

1. Begin your pot by making a base. Roll a small ball of the prepared clay in your hands. Press and pat it into a pancake. Make the base the same thickness all over. Thin spots will dry faster and can crack. Make the base about as thick as your little finger, between one-quarter and one-half inch (1/2 - 1 cm) thick. Smooth it carefully with your thumb. *(See diagram.)*

2. Use the needle tool to trim the pancake into a circle. The circle can be hand-sized or smaller. Fold up a little rim all around the edge. Let the base dry until it is firm but not too stiff. *(See diagram.)*

Coils

1. While the base is drying, begin to make the coils. Making good coils takes practice. Begin with a piece of prepared clay the size of a golf ball. Hold it in the air. Squeeze it and roll it gently between your hands so that it narrows at the bottom like a funnel. *(See diagram.)*

2. Continue to roll and squeeze the clay gently. A very thick rope of clay will begin to extend downward. Work slowly and concentrate on the feeling of the clay in your hands. Stop when the rope is about 5 inches (12 cm) long. *(See diagram.)*

3. Lay the rope of clay on the board. Roll it gently back and forth with your fingers to thin and lengthen it. Form a smooth, round coil that is the same thickness as your base. A good coil is an even thickness from one end to the other. This is hard to do! Keep your fingers spread wide. Slide them from the middle outward, and then back in. Keep practicing until you are satisfied. *(See diagram.)*

◄ Making the coils.

Make a Pot

1. Make a base.

2. Fold up a rim.

Coils

1. Begin a coil.

2. Make a rope of clay.

5 in. (12 cm)

3. Roll the coil.

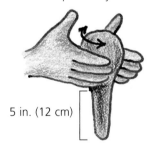

Shape the Pot

2. Join the coil to the base.

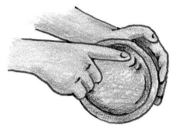

3. Add more coils.

4. Look at traditional Pueblo pot shapes.

Shape the Pot

1. Pick up the coil and lay it on the rim of your base. Make one loop around the rim, and then break the coil off. Push the two ends together.

2. Firmly join the coil to the base. Use your fingers, a wooden modeling tool, or a spoon handle. Scrape and blend the edges together on the inside and outside of the pot. Thin the walls out a little as you work, but not too much. It takes practice to judge how thin to scrape the walls. *(See diagram.)*

3. Make more coils and add them one at a time. Work slowly and carefully. If you rush, the walls of your pot will begin to be uneven, and it will be very hard to correct them. Pay attention to the feel of your clay. If the clay is too soft, your pot will sag and flop. If it is too dry, the coils won't stick together. *(See diagram.)*

4. Let the form of your pot grow. To make the wall of the pot open outward, add a slightly longer coil. To make the wall close inward, add a shorter coil. Look at traditional Pueblo pots for ideas. *(See diagram.)*

5. You may need to stop working before you are finished. Cover the top coil with a damp paper towel and a plastic bag. This will keep the clay workable.

6. Smooth out the sides of the pot some more. Gently pat the walls with your fingers to shape them. Examine your finished pot. Are the walls an even thickness? Is the shape pleasing? If you are not satisfied, enjoy the feeling of squashing the clay. Then start over!

7. If you are happy with your pot, set it aside to dry out partway. If the room temperature is warm, cover the pot loosely with plastic. This will slow the drying. Drying clay too fast often causes cracks to form. Check the pot daily. Turn it upside down to help it dry at the same rate all over.

8. When the pot is *leather hard,* stiff but not totally dry, it's ready to decorate.

Join the coil to the base ▶
with a modeling tool.

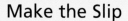

Make the Slip

1. You will decorate your pot with colored slip, or liquid clay. Make the slip with the same white clay that you used for your pot. This will ensure that the slip will fuse, or bond, with your pot when you fire it.

2. Break the clay into little pieces. Let it dry completely. It will take three or four days to dry. Don't stir up the dry clay or you will release dust into the air.

3. Put one cup (1/4 liter) of water into a large measuring cup. Drop bits of dry clay into the cup until the volume doubles. Let the clay sit overnight without stirring. It will dissolve into a creamy liquid. Use your fingers to squeeze out any lumps.

4. Divide the slip into three small plastic containers. Leave one portion white. Color the other portions red and black by adding ceramic stain. Use one ounce (30 g) of stain per one cup (1/4 liter) of slip. Slips differ, so you may need to adjust the stain for darkness. You will know after you fire your first pot.

Decorate Your Pot

1. The walls of your leather-hard pot should be firm enough to handle without bending. You can shape the pot a little more at this stage. Use a clay loop tool to carve off bits of clay. Smooth the walls with a piece of nylon window screen. **Wear a dust mask so you don't breathe the clay dust.** *(See diagram.)*

2. Use a thick paintbrush to coat the walls of your pot with slip. Try painting the outside one color and the inside a different color.

3. Let the slip dry for three or four minutes. Begin to *burnish,* or rub, the clay surface gently in little circles. Use a smooth stone or the back of a soupspoon. If the slip is too dry, you will scratch it with the stone. If the slip is too wet, it will stick to the stone and flake off. Continue to reapply the slip until you get the feel for it.

Stain Safety

Stains are made up of chemicals, such as chrome, iron, zinc, and aluminum oxide. Use good hygiene practices when mixing and using stains.

■ Wear a dust mask when you mix stains, and work in a well-ventilated area.

■ Don't eat while you're working with stains.

■ Avoid skin and eye contact.

■ Clean your worktable well when you are finished working.

Burnishing a pot. ▶

Decorate Your Pot

1. Shape the leather-hard pot.

5. Study Pueblo designs.

7. Draw guidelines on the slip.

4. Polish the slip until it begins to look shiny. Try stones of different sizes to get into all parts of the pot. If you want a plain pot, you can stop now.

5. It's fun to paint a design on your pot. The designs on Pueblo pots are often very complex. You will see lizards, birds, and many animals from myths. You will also see many geometric shapes that are symbols of things in nature. Study them to get ideas. *(See diagram.)*

6. Look your pot over and see if anything comes to mind. Pueblo potters say that the pot will tell them what to paint on it! Use an image that has a special meaning to you. You can draw the shape of your pot on paper and plan a design there.

7. Draw guidelines on the slip with charcoal, or use your fingernail to mark the design. Use a fine brush to paint your design with slip. Then set the pot aside to dry. Be very careful not to scratch or nick the slip. *(See diagram.)*

8. When the clay no longer feels cool to the touch, it's ready to fire. Fire your pot in a kiln at cone 06 (1873° F/1023° C).

9. When fired, the burnished, or rubbed, areas will have a gloss and the painted areas will be dull. Because your pot is fired at a low temperature, it will be fragile. It will also soak up water, so don't use it for food or liquids.

Other Ideas

■ Carve a design into the wall of the pot at the leather-hard stage. You will need to make a pot with very thick walls for this decorating method.

■ Try scratching designs through the colored slip after burnishing. The color of the white clay will show through.

Students' finished ▶ coil pots.

Glossary

abalone a marine mollusk with an ear-shaped shell. The colorful, pearly interior of the shell is often used for making jewelry and ornaments.

abstract having a quality or meaning beyond the actual object

adobe a sun-dried brick made of clay and straw

Anglo Caucasian, or white, person living in the United States

appliquéd cut out and sewn onto a larger piece of material

archipelago a group of islands

artisans people who are skilled in an art, a craft, or a trade

butte a steep mountain or hill rising sharply above nearby land

button blanket ceremonial robe worn by Northwest Coast Indians

conjuring calling up spirits or using magical arts

crop rotation the practice of planting different crops in the same soil

crest identifying symbol or ornament

decoy an artifical bird, often formed from wood, used by hunters to attract a real bird to a place within shooting range

extinction the process of the dying out of a species of animal, plant, or a group of people

immigrants people who enter and settle in a region that is not their native home

intolerance an unwillingness to allow or permit differences in opinions or beliefs, including religious beliefs

kiva a round chamber where Pueblo Indians hold ceremonies

mesa a flat-topped mountain or hill

persecution ill-treatment or oppression of someone, especially on the basis of race, religion, or beliefs

petrified changed over time into stone

potlatch a ceremony of Northwest Coast Indians involving the giving away of important gifts. Gifts are given in return some-time in the future.

shale a rock with many layers of fine particles of clay, mud, or silt

stalactite a deposit of calcium carbonate that looks like an icicle hanging from the roof or sides of a cavern, or cave

stalagmite a deposit of calcium carbonate and water that drips down on the floor of a cave to form a rough cone shape

symmetrical balanced or even in form

totem pole tall pillar carved and painted with symbols by Northwest Coast Indians

whittled a piece of wood shaped by paring or cutting off chips from its surface with a knife

yucca a plant, found in the southwestern United States, that has long, stiff leaves

Abbreviations Key

C	Centigrade
cm	centimeters
F	Fahrenheit
ft.	feet
g	grams
in.	inches
km	kilometers
m	meters
mi.	miles
oz.	ounce
sq.	square
yd.	yard

Resources

Queen Charlotte Islands

Aja, Christopher. *The Sea Monster: A Tale from the Pacific Northwest.* San Diego, CA: Harcourt Brace, 1999

Davidson, Robert. *Eagle Transforming: The Art of Robert Davidson.* Seattle: University of Washington Press, 1994

Jensen, Doreen, and Polly Sargent. *Robes of Power: Totem Poles on Cloth.* Vancouver: University of British Columbia Press, 1986

MacDonald, George F. *Haida Art.* Seattle: University of Washington Press, 1998

Pennsylvania

Doherty, Kieran. *William Penn: Quaker Colonist.* Brookfield, CT: Millbrook, 1998

Pellow, Randall A. and Lucille Wallower. *Pennsylvania Geography: The Keystone State.* Landsdale, PA: Penns Valley, 1995

Shea, John G. *The Pennsylvania Dutch and Their Furniture.* New York: Van Nostrand Reinhold, 1980

Swain, Gwenyth. *Pennsylvania.* Minneapolis, MN: Lerner, 1994

Southern United States

Anderson, June. *Honoring the Ancestors: The Woodcarvings of Claude Lockhart Clark.* Seattle: University of Washington Press, 1997

Hoig, Stan. *Night of the Cruel Moon: Cherokee Removal and the Trail of Tears.* New York: Facts on File, 1996

McGuire, Kevin. *Woodworking for Kids: 40 Fabulous, Fun, and Useful Things for Kids to Make.* Pittsburgh, PA: Sterling, 1993

Meyers, Madeleine. *Cherokee Nation: Life Before the Tears,* "Perspectives on History" series. Carlisle, MA: Discovery Enterprises, 1993

Roberts, Norma. *Elijah Pierce, Woodcarver.* Columbus, OH: Columbus Museum of Art, 1992

New Mexico

Baldwin, Louis. *Intruders Within: Pueblo Resistance to Spanish Rule and the Revolt of 1680,* "American Indian Experience" series. New York: Watts, 1995

Cordell, Linda. *Ancient Pueblo Peoples,* "Exploring the Ancient World" series. Washington, DC: Smithsonian, 1995

Dillingham, Rick. *Fourteen Families in Pueblo Pottery.* Albuquerque: University of New Mexico Press, 1994

Philip, Neil. *In a Sacred Manner I Live.* New York: Clarion, 1997

Ross, Pamela. *The Pueblo Indians,* "Native Peoples" series. Mankato, MN: Capstone, 1999

Wood, Nancy, ed. *The Serpent's Tongue: Prose, Poetry, and Art of the New Mexican Pueblos.* New York: NAL-Dutton, 1997

Index

Acknowledgments

Special thanks to these students for making the project samples: Andrew, Breeze, Cameron, Carlye, Carrie B., Carrie S., Louis, Melinda, Tim, and Quail; and to Arius, Jessica, Lok, Sarah, and Tyler for their help. Thanks to Jefferson Middle School, Eugene, Oregon; Christie Newland; Lynn Pedersen; Rockey Sigloh; Diane Cissel, Terragraphics; Libris Solar; Percy Franklin; Stephen Reynolds; and Wade Long. Special thanks to Robert Davidson.